POCKET MANUAL
SHARKS

First published in 2007.
This edition published in October 2019.

David G. Thompson MSc has asserted his right to be identified as the author of this book.

British Library Cataloguing-in-Publication Data:
A catalogue record for this book is available
from the British Library

ISBN 978 1 78521 676 3

Library of Congress catalog card no. 2019942928

Design by Richard Parsons and James Robertson

Published by Haynes Publishing, Sparkford, Yeovil, Somerset BA22 7JJ, UK
Tel: +44 (0)1963 440635
Website: www.haynes.com

Haynes North America, Inc., 859 Lawrence Drive, Newbury Park, California 91320, USA

Printed in Malaysia

Photographic credits:
Erika Yves Antoniazzo: p164; Dray van Beeck: p42, 86, 88, 118-124, 150, 168; Dan Bolt: p154, 156; Paul vander Eecken: p62-68; David B. Fleetham: p34-40, 114, 116; Saul Gonor/seapics.com: p84; Daniel W. Gotshall/seapics.com: p128; Marion Haarsma: p60; Tom Haught/seapics.com: p102; Dean Innell: p172; Dennis King: p18, 20; Gwen Lowe/seapics.com: p54, 56; Randy Morse: p110, 112; Andy Murch: p12, 52, 76, 138, 140, 180; Doug Perrine/seapics.com: p178; Bruce Rasna/seapics.com: p104; David Shen/seapics.com: p70, 72; Marty Snyderman/seapics.com: p130, 132; David Thompson: p16, 24, 30, 32, 96, 100, 102, 104, 108, 136, 144, 152, 182, 184; Cary Yany: 160; Murat Zayim: p176

The Author

David Thompson is an experienced dive instructor and a qualified marine biologist. His work has taken him around the world and involved him in many aspects of marine conservation. He has a particular passion for sharks and his dream is to dive with Great Whites...without a cage!

POCKET MANUAL
SHARKS

Haynes

Contents

About this book

This exciting book features 45 sharks from around the
world, from basking sharks, tiger sharks and hammerheads
to the enormous whale shark and the infamous and much
maligned great white. Packed with fascinating facts, stunning
photographs and all the vital statistics, this is the essential
pocket guide. We've also included a useful introduction to
shark anatomy and terminology so you can learn even more
about these fascinating creatures.

Shark anatomy

An introduction

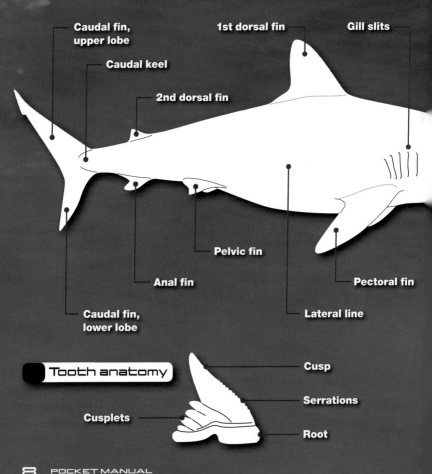

- Caudal fin, upper lobe
- Caudal keel
- 2nd dorsal fin
- 1st dorsal fin
- Gill slits
- Pelvic fin
- Anal fin
- Caudal fin, lower lobe
- Lateral line
- Pectoral fin

Tooth anatomy

- Cusp
- Serrations
- Cusplets
- Root

Scientific terminology

Reproduction

Viviparous	Shark gives birth to live pups that have developed inside the womb
Oviparous	Shark lays egg cases that hatch independently from the mother
Ovoviviparous	Shark produces eggs, which remain inside the body, where they hatch
Uterine cannibalism	The first pups to develop or hatch eat the remaining eggs/embryos or other pups in the womb

Taxonomy

Crustaceans	Crabs, lobsters, prawns and shrimps
Molluscs	Mussels, snails, and other snail-like animals that live in a shell
Cephalopods	Octopus and squid
Invertebrates	Animals without a backbone
Bony fish	All fish other than sharks and rays
Batoids	Flat sharks, otherwise known as rays

Habitat

Pelagic	Open ocean dwelling
Continental shelf	The shallow depths around the coasts of continents, which can extend many miles out to sea
Benthic	Lives on the bottom of the sea either on or in the sediment/sand

Mouth

Eye and spiracle behind

Nostril

Snout

Basking shark

Cetorhinus maximus

Basking shark

Cetorhinus maximus

This is the second-largest shark and has a huge mouth and gill slits that almost surround the head. It has a pointed snout and tiny hooked teeth. It filters plankton on the surface at tidal water fronts and relies on movement to push the plankton through its gills. Basking sharks often swim together in intricate patterns when feeding and sometimes they spring entirely out of the water (breaching) to try to dislodge parasites. They are found in cold to warm coastal waters, but migrate to deeper, offshore waters in winter. The female produces a large number of eggs inside her, which hatch gradually and the first hatchlings then eat the remaining eggs (uterine cannibalism) but not each other. Basking sharks are harmless to humans and will approach boats without fear.

Statistics

Common name	**Basking shark**
Family	**Basking sharks**
Size at birth	**Possibly 1.5–1.7m**
Maximum size	**12–15m**
Maximum weight	**4,000kg**
Maturity at	**Male 4–7m** **Female 8–10m**
Reproduction	**Ovoviviparous with uterine cannibalism**
Litter size	**1–6**
Food	**Plankton, krill and possibly other small fish**
Top speed	**3.9kph**
Teeth count	**1,000+**
Depth	**0–2,000m**

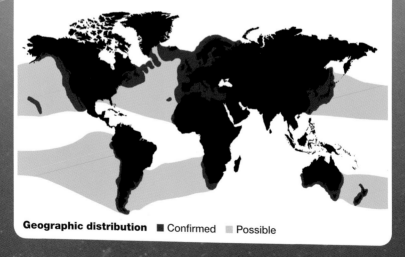

Geographic distribution ■ Confirmed ■ Possible

Blacktail Reef shark

Carcharhinus wheeleri

Blacktail Reef shark

Carcharhinus wheeleri

The Blacktail Reef is a medium, stocky grey shark with a fairly long and broadly rounded snout. It has a broad black band on its tail, second dorsal and anal fins, and a white tip on the first dorsal fin. Its teeth are narrow and triangular with serrated edges and cusplets in the upper jaw, and very narrow and serrated in the lower jaw. This shark is often confused with the grey reef shark and scientists are still arguing about whether it is the same species. Blacktail Reef sharks can be found mainly on coral reefs, coastal drop-offs and deeper banks offshore, although the younger ones prefer shallower water. They feed on small reef fish, squid and octopus. The female gives birth to between one and four live young. Although usually harmless to humans, the Blacktail Reef shark can become aggressive if spear fishing activities are taking place nearby, and therefore it is classed as potentially dangerous.

Common name	Blacktail Reef shark
Family	Requiem sharks
Size at birth	65–70cm
Maximum size	1.7–1.9m
Maximum weight	34kg
Maturity at	Male 1.1–1.3m Female 1.2–1.4m
Reproduction	Viviparous
Litter size	1–4
Food	Small reef fish, squid and octopus
Top speed	45kph
Teeth count	50–56
Depth	0–140m

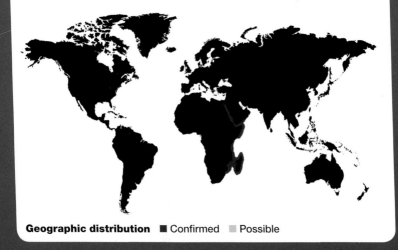

Geographic distribution ■ Confirmed ■ Possible

Blacktip shark

Carcharhinus limbatus

Blacktip shark

Carcharhinus limbatus

The Blacktip is a moderately large, stocky grey shark with a fairly long and pointed snout. It has black tips on all its fins except the upper tail fin, and it should not be confused with the smaller Blacktip Reef shark. Its upper teeth are narrow and triangular with serrated edges, and its lower teeth are very narrow and serrated. It can be found worldwide in tropical and sub-tropical continental waters and sometimes in pelagic waters, although it is not a true ocean-dwelling shark. Blacktips often congregate in large groups just under the surface. They are very active swimmers and sometimes leap completely out of the water. They feed on bony reef fish, squid, octopus and crustaceans. Although usually harmless to humans, if annoyed, Blacktips will attack, although no reports of attacks exist.

Common name	**Blacktip shark**
Family	**Requiem sharks**
Size at birth	**38–72cm**
Maximum size	**2.3–2.6m**
Maximum weight	**123kg**
Maturity at	**Male 1.4–1.8m** **Female 1.2–1.9m**
Reproduction	**Viviparous**
Litter size	**1–10**
Food	**Bony reef fish, squid, octopus and crustaceans**
Top speed	**23kph**
Teeth count	**60–64**
Depth	**0–30m**

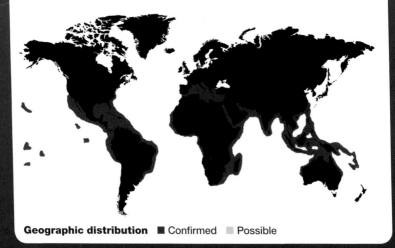

Geographic distribution ■ Confirmed ■ Possible

Blacktip Reef shark

Carcharhinus melanopterus

Blacktip Reef shark

Carcharhinus melanopterus

The Blacktip Reef is a medium, stocky grey-brown shark with black tips on all fins, with the black marks on the first dorsal and lower tail fins being larger and more vivid. It has a small, pointed snout, oval eyes and a white belly. The upper jaw teeth are narrow and pointed with serrated edges and cusplets. The lower jaw teeth are tall, pointed and slightly serrated. Blacktip Reefs are found in the Red Sea and Indo-Pacific in tropical shallow inshore waters and coral reefs. They have now entered the eastern Mediterranean Sea through the Suez Canal, and can also be found in rivers and lakes in Madagascar, but cannot remain for extended periods in fresh water. Young Blacktip Reefs are often found under jetties in very shallow water. They feed on fish, cephalopods and crustaceans. They are generally harmless to humans.

Common name	**Blacktip Reef shark**
Family	**Requiem sharks**
Size at birth	**33–53cm**
Maximum size	**1.6–1.9m**
Maximum weight	**14kg**
Maturity at	**Male 1.3–1.8m** **Female 96–112cm**
Reproduction	**Viviparous**
Litter size	**2–4**
Food	**Fish, crustaceans and cephalopods**
Top speed	**Unknown**
Teeth count	**42–50**
Depth	**0–35m**

Geographic distribution ■ Confirmed ■ Possible

Blue shark

Prionacea glauca

Blue shark

Prionacea glauca

This is a large, slender torpedo-shaped shark with a dark blue back, light blue sides, white belly, a long snout and large eyes. The teeth are broadly triangular and serrated in the upper jaw and narrow and pointed in the lower jaw. It is found worldwide in temperate oceanic waters but can also be found in tropical waters, but at much greater depths. The Blue is a very fast shark and generally swims with the dorsal fin and tail tip out of the water. It eats mainly squid, either by darting through large schools and grabbing lots of squid at once, or by standing on its tail and picking squid out of the school. It also eats small fish, sharks, crustaceans and carrion. The Blue shark is potentially dangerous to humans.

Common name	**Blue shark**
Family	**Requiem sharks**
Size at birth	**35–44cm**
Maximum size	**3.8–4m**
Maximum weight	**206kg**
Maturity at	**Male 1.8–2.8m**
	Female 2.2–3.2m
Reproduction	**Viviparous**
Litter size	**3–130**
Food	**Squid, fish, octopus, crustaceans, carrion and smaller sharks**
Top speed	**39.4kph**
Teeth count	**49–65**
Depth	**0–150m in temperate (7–17°C)**
	75–220m in tropical (12–25°C)

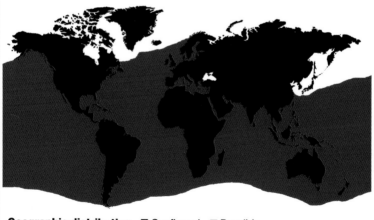

Geographic distribution ■ Confirmed ■ Possible

Bluespotted Stingray

Taeniura lymma

Bluespotted Stingray

Taeniura lymma

This is a stingray and therefore not a true shark; it is a small batoid-shark with a grey-yellow to olive-green body and bright blue spots on its disc-shaped body and blue bands along the sides of its tail. It has a poisonous spine positioned much further back on its tail than it is on most rays and the tail is nearly twice the body length. The teeth are two 'plates' adapted for crushing the shells of its food, and it eats molluscs, crustaceans and polychaetes. It is found on tropical coral reefs of the Indo-Pacific Ocean, Red Sea, Asia and Australia. Unlike most rays, the Bluespotted Stingray rarely buries itself in the sand. It is harmless to humans unless provoked. Then it will lash out with its spine and the poison can be very painful. The barb of the spine is so big that people have bled to death from the wound.

Statistics

Common name	**Bluespotted Stingray**
Family	**Fantail rays**
Size at birth	**10–13cm**
Maximum size	**70–90cm long and 30cm wide**
Maximum weight	**3kg**
Maturity at	**Male 37–40cm** **Female 45–50cm**
Reproduction	**Ovoviviparous**
Litter size	**1–7**
Food	**Molluscs, crustaceans and polychaetes**
Top speed	**Unknown**
Teeth count	**2**
Depth	**2–30m**

Geographic distribution ■ Confirmed ■ Possible

Bluntnose Sixgill shark

Hexanchus griseus

Bluntnose Sixgill shark

Hexanchus griseus

Common name	**Bluntnose Sixgill shark**
Family	**Cow sharks**
Size at birth	**65–70cm**
Maximum size	**4.8–5m**
Maximum weight	**590kg**
Maturity at	**Male 4–4.5m** **Female 4.4–4.8m**
Reproduction	**Ovoviviparous**
Litter size	**100–110**
Food	**Fish, sharks, rays, squid, seals, crustaceans and carrion**
Top speed	**Unknown**
Teeth count	**26–30**
Depth	**0 to at least 1,870m**

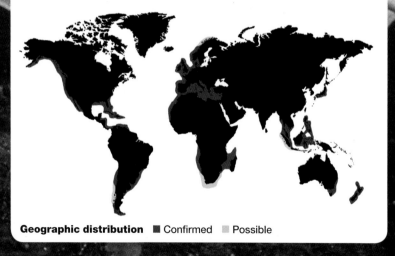

Geographic distribution ■ Confirmed ■ Possible

Bronze Whaler shark
or Copper shark
Carcharhinus brachyurus

Bronze Whaler shark
or Copper shark
Carcharhinus brachyurus

The Bronze Whaler or Copper shark gets its name from the copper sheen of its body in sunlight. This is a large, grey-bronze-coloured shark with a fairly long, broadly rounded snout. The pelvic and pectoral fins have darker tips and the underside is pale to white. Its teeth are hooked, narrow and pointed with serrated edges in the upper jaw, and narrower and straighter in the lower jaw. They are found in warm temperate to sub-tropical waters both inshore and offshore along the coasts of South Africa, Australia, Japan, South America, Baja California, north-western Africa and the Mediterranean. They can also be found in large coastal bays. The Bronze Whaler feeds on pelagic and bottom-dwelling bony fish, small sharks, rays and cephalopods. It is potentially dangerous and has been involved in attacks on divers. This is a popular shark for sports fishermen.

Statistics

Common name	**Bronze Whaler shark or Copper shark**
Family	**Requiem sharks**
Size at birth	**60–70cm**
Maximum size	**2.9–3.5m**
Maximum weight	**305kg**
Maturity at	**Male 2–2.3m** **Female 2.2–2.4m**
Reproduction	**Viviparous**
Litter size	**12–20**
Food	**Pelagic and bottom-dwelling bony fish,** **small sharks, rays, squid and octopus**
Top speed	**Unknown**
Teeth count	**56–62**
Depth	**0–110mm**

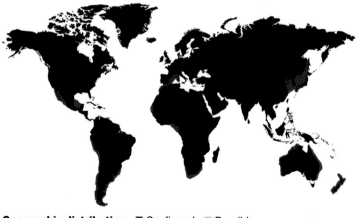

Geographic distribution ■ Confirmed ■ Possible

Bull shark

Carcharhinus leucas

Bull shark

Carcharhinus leucas

This is a stocky grey shark with few distinctive markings, a short, broadly rounded snout and small eyes. It has broad triangular serrated teeth in the upper jaw and narrower smooth teeth in the lower jaw. Bull sharks are very common, being found in coastal tropical and sub-tropical waters and estuaries, mostly in very shallow water. They will also swim hundreds of kilometres upriver and they can live in both freshwater and salty lakes, but only if they have access to the sea. Like Tiger sharks, they will eat anything – marine mammals, fish, rays, sharks and birds – and have been known to attack domestic animals wading in shallow water at river banks. The Bull shark is extremely dangerous to humans. It is number three in the shark attack files, but because of its size, lack of distinctive features and the fact it's found everywhere, many attacks not thought to be by this shark should be. It is probably more dangerous than the Great White.

Common name	**Bull shark**
Family	**Requiem sharks**
Size at birth	**56–81cm**
Maximum size	**3.4m**
Maximum weight	**316kg**
Maturity at	**Male 1.6–2.3m** **Female 1.8–2.3m**
Reproduction	**Viviparous**
Litter size	**1–13**
Food	**Fish, sharks and rays, crustaceans, molluscs, sea birds, turtles, dolphins, small whales, reptiles, dogs and other domestic animals**
Top speed	**19kph**
Teeth count	**48–52**
Depth	**0–152m**

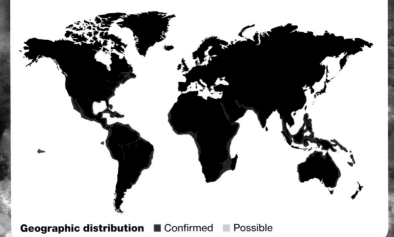

Geographic distribution ■ Confirmed ■ Possible

Caribbean Reef shark

Carcharhinus perezi

Caribbean Reef shark

Carcharhinus perezi

The Caribbean Reef is a large, stocky, grey shark with a fairly short, broadly rounded snout, a yellowish-white belly and large eyes. The first dorsal fin is quite large, although the second dorsal is small compared to that of other grey sharks, and the large, narrow pectoral fins have dark tips underneath. The upper teeth are narrow, slightly oblique (curved at the tip) and pointed with serrated edges while the lower teeth are narrower and straighter. This is the most common reef shark in the Caribbean, found also in the Bahamas and parts of the western Atlantic, living on the tropical coral reefs in quite shallow water. Throughout the Caribbean, these sharks are very popular as they are always around at shark-feeding dives. They eat fish, small sharks, rays and cephalopods, and although generally harmless to humans they have been involved in attacks on divers.

Statistics

Common name	**Caribbean Reef shark**
Family	**Requiem sharks**
Size at birth	**65–70cm**
Maximum size	**2.7–2.9m**
Maximum weight	**70kg**
Maturity at	**Male 1.5–1.7m** **Female 2.2–2.4m**
Reproduction	**Viviparous**
Litter size	**4–6**
Food	**Reef fish, small sharks, rays, squid and octopus**
Top speed	**Unknown**
Teeth count	**44–52**
Depth	**0–40m**

Geographic distribution ■ Confirmed ■ Possible

Chimaera
or Spotted Ratfish
Hydrolagus colliei **(water rabbit)**

Chimaera
or Spotted Ratfish
Hydrolagus colliei **(water rabbit)**

This is not a true shark but a close relative. It is small, with a large, rabbit-like face, a flat, duckbill snout and a door-knocker-shaped organ on its forehead, which it uses to hold on to the female while mating. It has a poisonous spine on the first dorsal fin, large wing-like pectoral fins and the tail is half as long as the body and tapered. The Chimaera is silvery bronze with white spots, and it has large, emerald green eyes that light up in the dark and large rabbit-like teeth. It is found in the eastern Pacific from Southern Alaska to Baja California in deep temperate waters and is nocturnal (active at night). It eats crustaceans, shellfish and snails. The female lays two violin-shaped eggs, which takes 18–30 hours, and these are then dragged behind her for four to six days before they catch on the bottom. The Chimaera does not attack humans, but the poisonous spine and the vicious teeth can cause painful injuries.

Common name	**Chimaera or Spotted Ratfish or Ghostfish**
Family	**Short-nose chimaeras**
Size at birth	**10cm**
Maximum size	**97–101cm**
Maximum weight	**Unknown**
Maturity at	**Male unknown** **Female unknown**
Reproduction	**Oviparous**
Litter size	**2**
Food	**Crustaceans, shellfish and gastropods**
Top speed	**Unknown**
Teeth count	**Unknown**
Depth	**2–1,000m**

Geographic distribution ■ Confirmed ▨ Possible

Cookie-cutter shark

Isistius brasiliensis

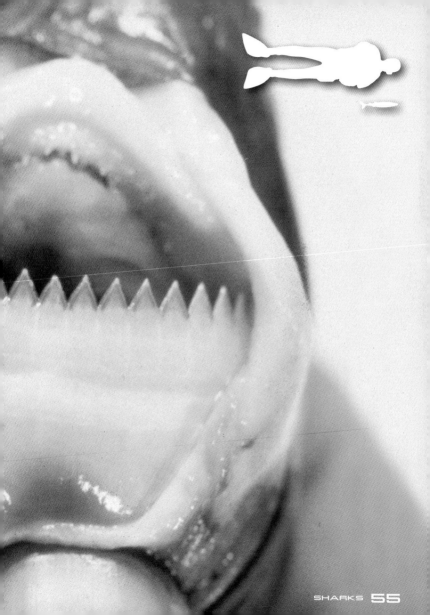

Cookie-cutter shark

Isistius brasiliensis

This is a very small, cigar-shaped shark with a rounded
snout, spineless dorsal fins and is dark brown in colour with
a dark band around its neck. The teeth are small and pointed
in the upper jaw, and huge and triangular in the lower jaw.
The Cookie-cutter gets its name because it attaches itself to
its victim by suction with its lips and then spins, cutting out
a round plug of flesh with its lower teeth. Plug-holes have
been found in whales, big sharks, dolphins and other marine
mammals. The Latin name comes from Isis, the goddess of
light – its body lights up in the dark, possibly to attract larger
fish so it can attack them. Cookie-cutters are found in various
spots around the world, in very deep water during the day
and coming to the surface only at night. They are harmless to
humans, but if swimming at night then a bite is possible.

Common name	Cookie-cutter shark
Family	Sleeper sharks
Size at birth	Unknown
Maximum size	45–50cm
Maximum weight	Unknown
Maturity at	Male 31–37cm Female 38–44cm
Reproduction	Ovoviviparous
Litter size	6–8
Food	Flesh from fish, sharks, rays and marine mammals, squid. It has also been known to bite submarines, especially the rubber radar domes!
Top speed	Unknown
Teeth count	55–68
Depth	0 to at least 1,000m

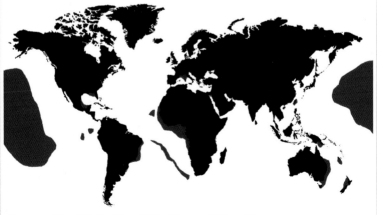

Geographic distribution ■ Confirmed ▨ Possible

Coral Catshark

Atelomycterus marmoratus

Coral Catshark

Atelomycterus marmoratus

This is a small, slender catshark with a narrow head, extended nasal flaps and nasal grooves. The male has very long, thin claspers, which are unique to this species. The body is pale cream, forming large white dots with dark edges and with a dark pattern of marks and patches of different colours but no clear saddle markings. It has tricuspid (three-pointed) teeth with the middle cusp being twice as large as the outer cusps. It is found on coral reefs in the shallow tropical waters of the Indo-West Pacific Ocean and Asian seas, and lives in crevices and holes, where it hides during the day. It is thought to be nocturnal and is a very active hunter, preying on small fish, squid, mussels and snails. It is harmless to humans, but is caught by humans and eaten either fresh or salt-dried or processed as fish meal.

Common name	**Coral Catshark**
Family	**Catsharks**
Size at birth	**10–12cm**
Maximum size	**65–70cm**
Maximum weight	**Unknown**
Maturity at	**Male 45–50cm** **Female 49–57cm**
Reproduction	**Oviparous**
Litter size	**1 egg case per ovary**
Food	**Small bony fish and larvae, squid, mussels and snails**
Top speed	**Unknown**
Teeth count	**Unknown**
Depth	**0.5–15m (possibly deeper)**

Geographic distribution ■ Confirmed ■ Possible

Galapagos shark

Carcharhinus galapagensis

Galapagos shark

Carcharhinus galapagensis

This is a very large and slender grey shark with a long, broad snout and fairly large eyes. It is very similar in shape and size to other grey sharks in its area, but can be distinguished by a slightly larger first dorsal fin compared with the others. Its teeth are broad and triangular with heavily serrated, slightly oblique (curved) cusps in the upper jaw, while in the lower jaw they are narrow, tall and serrated. Galapagos sharks are found worldwide in tropical waters and prefer oceanic islands, but can also be found along the coasts of Baja California, Columbia and Guatemala and rarely in open oceans. However, young sharks prefer shallower waters, unlike adults. They feed mainly on bottom-dwelling fish, squid, octopus and eels and experiments have shown that they prefer fish to crab meat . This shark poses a dangerous risk to humans.

Common name	Galapagos shark
Family	Requiem sharks
Size at birth	57–80cm
Maximum size	3.2–3.6m
Maximum weight	85kg
Maturity at	Male 1.7–2.3m Female 2.2–2.4m
Reproduction	Viviparous
Litter size	5–15
Food	Bottom-dwelling fish, squid, eels and octopus
Top speed	At least 3.2kph
Teeth count	52–60
Depth	0–190m (young max. depth 20–25m)

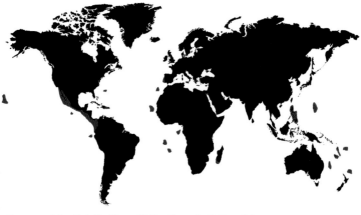

Geographic distribution ■ Confirmed ■ Possible

Galapagos Bullhead
or Peruvian Horn shark
Heterodontus quoyi

Galapagos Bullhead
or Peruvian Horn shark
Heterodontus quoyi

This is a very small shark with a round body, a cone-shaped head and a pig-like nose. It has spines on both dorsal fins and has large pectoral fins. The body is a light brown to grey colour with large black spots over the entire body. Its teeth are molar-shaped (rather than pointed) in order to grind the shell of its prey, but it also has gripping teeth in front. This is a nocturnal shark that lives in inshore continental and island waters on sand flats and rocky reef areas with sandy patches. Found only in Peru and the Galapagos Islands – hence its name – the Galapagos Bullhead often lies very still on the sand during the day and is a very poor swimmer. It feeds mainly on crabs but is also believed to eat shellfish and snails. It is harmless to humans.

Statistics

Common name	**Galapagos Bullhead or Peruvian Horn shark**
Family	**Bullhead sharks**
Size at birth	**16–17cm**
Maximum size	**60–61cm**
Maximum weight	**Unknown**
Maturity at	**Male 45–48cm** **Female 46–50cm?**
Reproduction	**Oviparous**
Litter size	**Unknown**
Food	**Mainly crabs, but also gastropods, snails and polychaetes**
Top speed	**Unknown**
Teeth count	**20–30**
Depth	**3–40m**

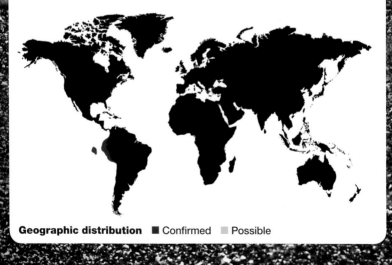

Geographic distribution ■ Confirmed ■ Possible

Goblin shark

Mitsukurina owstoni

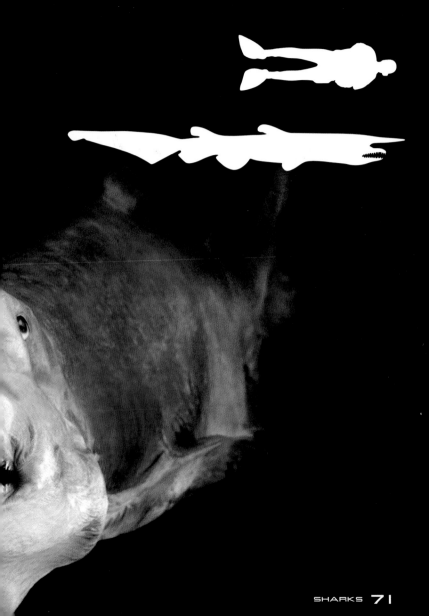

Goblin shark

Mitsukurina owstoni

The Goblin shark is a living fossil. Many sharks were similar to this one 200 million years ago, but now there are only a few species left. It is a large and unique shark with a very long tail, rounded fins and a large sword-like extended snout. The snout may be used to detect prey in the dark waters of the deep. It is pinkish-white in colour and the jaws can be extended far forward. Its teeth are long and pointed (dagger-shaped) and decrease in size towards the back of the mouth, finally becoming molar-shaped. It is found in deep waters worldwide, but is very rare and most records are from Portugal and Japan. It eats fish and squid, which it catches by shooting its jaws forwards, and may also eat crustaceans – hence the crushing molars at the back of the mouth. It is harmless to humans.

Common name	**Goblin shark**
Family	**Goblin sharks**
Size at birth	**Less than 1m**
Maximum size	**3.8–4m**
Maximum weight	**Unknown**
Maturity at	**Male 2.6–3.2m** **Female 3–3.2m**
Reproduction	**Unknown**
Litter size	**Unknown**
Food	**Fish and squid, maybe also crustaceans**
Top speed	**Unknown**
Teeth count	**84–88**
Depth	**?–1,500m (not believed to enter shallow water)**

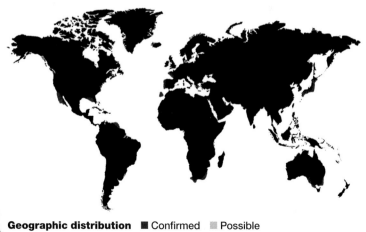

Geographic distribution ■ Confirmed ■ Possible

Great Hammerhead

Sphyrna mokarran

Great Hammerhead

Sphyrna mokarran

This hammerhead is easily recognised as a very large shark with a huge first dorsal fin and an almost straight front edge to its hammer, which is extended far in front of its gills. The front teeth are long and broad with heavily serrated edges and the back teeth are almost molar-shaped. It is found worldwide in tropical coastal and semi-oceanic waters, preferring continental and island coral reefs, although it appears to move towards the poles in the summer. It feeds on rays, batoid fish, fish, squid and other sharks. It seems to be immune to the stings from stingrays – one was found with more than 50 stings stuck in its mouth and tongue! Although not an agressive shark, the Great Hammerhead is dangerous because it is fearless and eats almost anything.

Common name	**Great (or Giant) Hammerhead shark**
Family	**Hammerhead sharks**
Size at birth	**50–70cm**
Maximum size	**5.5–6.2m (males usually only 3.5m)**
Maximum weight	**450kg**
Maturity at	**Male 2.3–2.7m**
	Female 2.5–3m
Reproduction	**Viviparous**
Litter size	**13–42 in litter**
Food	**Fish, squid, octopus, rays and other batoids, other sharks**
Top speed	**40kph**
Teeth count	**69–80**
Depth	**0–80m**

Geographic distribution ■ Confirmed ■ Possible

Great White shark

Carcharodon carcharias

Great White shark

Carcharodon carcharias

This is a huge spindle-shaped shark with a white belly and a grey to blackish-grey upper body. It has a long pointed snout and very distinctive black eyes. The teeth are large, flat, triangular and saw-like with serrated edges. The Great White can be found in most waters worldwide, but mostly in cooler temperate waters. It prefers coasts and offshore islands, but has also been spotted in the open ocean. It is an active swimmer, cruising at about 1.6–3.2 kilometres per hour, but will produce very fast sprints and even spring completely out of the water. It eats marine mammals (including small whales), reptiles, birds, sharks, fish, crustaceans and squid. The female produces 2–14 egg cases, which hatch inside her and uterine cannibalism is common. The mother stops eating during the pupping period so as not to eat her own young. The Great White is number one in the shark attack files although it is more likely that most attacks were by the Tiger shark.

Common name	Great White shark
Family	Mackerel sharks
Size at birth	1.1–1.7m
Maximum size	6–7m
Maximum weight	3,400kg
Maturity at	Male 3.5–4.1m Female 4–5m
Reproduction	Ovoviviparous
Litter size	2–14
Food	Marine mammals, reptiles, birds, fish, crustaceans, sharks and carrion
Top speed	40kph
Teeth count	50–60
Depth	0–1,280m

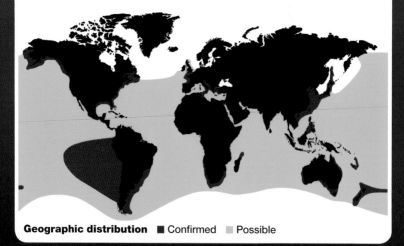

Geographic distribution ■ Confirmed ■ Possible

Greenland shark

Somniosus microcephalus

Greenland shark

Somniosus microcephalus

The Greenland shark is a large, sluggish shark with a short snout, cylindrical body and no anal fins. The dorsal fins are very small, spineless and positioned far back on the body. The teeth are spear-shaped in the upper jaw, and short and broad with oblique (curved) cusps in the lower jaw. All of the teeth are razor sharp and are used by Eskimos as knives. It is found in cold Arctic and North Atlantic waters from the shallows down to at least 1,250 metres. It has a unique copepod parasite (a shrimp-like animal) attached to each eye that glows in the dark. These are believed to attract fish so the shark can catch them. It eats almost anything, but its main diet is fish, although it will eat marine mammals and any carrion it can find. It is considered harmless to humans , although some Eskimo legends tell of it attacking boats.

Common name	Greenland shark
Family	Sleeper sharks
Size at birth	37cm
Maximum size	6.5–7m
Maximum weight	775kg
Maturity at	Male 3.4–3.6m Female 4.8–5m
Reproduction	Ovoviviparous
Litter size	Approximately 10
Food	Fish, skates, seals, dead whales and any other carrion
Top speed	At least 1.2kph
Teeth count	98–104
Depth	0–1250m

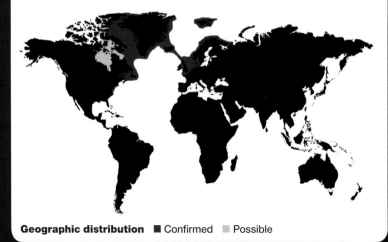

Geographic distribution ■ Confirmed ■ Possible

Giant Guitarfish
or Sharkfin ray
Rhynchobatus djiddensis

Giant Guitarfish

or Sharkfin ray

Rhynchobatus djiddensis

This is not a true shark but a ray, although it is often mistaken for a shark because it has the tail and dorsal fins of a shark and swims like one, too. The gills are positioned underneath, the pectoral fins are fused to the head and the snout is elongated like a dolphin's. The upper body is olive to grey and juveniles have white spots, which gradually fade as they become adults. The teeth are flattened pavement-shaped, and are used to crush the shells of prey. The Giant Guitarfish is found in the Indo-Pacific, Red Sea and around Australia in tropical inshore waters and in slightly salty lagoons. It is often seen resting on sandy bottoms perched on its fins with its head off the bottom pumping water through its gills. It feeds on crustaceans, gastropods, cephalopods, fish and mussels. It is harmless to humans.

Common name	**Giant Guitarfish or Sharkfin ray**
Family	**Guitar fish**
Size at birth	**60cm**
Maximum size	**2.8–3.1m**
Maximum weight	**227kg**
Maturity at	**Male 1.5–1.56m**
	Female 1.6–1.77m
Reproduction	**Ovoviviparous**
Litter size	**4–10**
Food	**Bony fish, crustaceans, bivalves and cephalopods**
Top speed	**At least 2kph**
Teeth count	**20–30**
Depth	**2–50m**

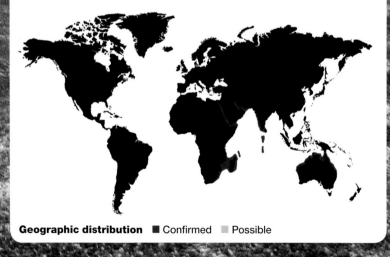

Geographic distribution ■ Confirmed ▣ Possible

Lemon shark

Negaprion brevirostris

Lemon shark

Negaprion brevirostris

This is a large, stocky yellow-brown shark that has a short nose and a second dorsal fin almost as big as the first. Its upper teeth are narrow, pointed and serrated at the base, and the lower teeth are smooth. It is an abundant species found in tropical coastal waters of the northern part of South America, Central America, the Caribbean, the east coast of the USA, Baja California and the Gulf of Mexico, and it can also be found on the Ivory Coast and Senegal. Although preferring mangroves, coral reefs, docks and river estuaries, it will enter fresh water, but not very far. It eats mainly fish and rays, but sometimes also crustaceans, molluscs and, very rarely, sea birds. The Lemon shark is potentially dangerous to humans and has been reported to attack swimmers and boats when disturbed.

Common name	**Lemon shark**
Family	**Requiem sharks**
Size at birth	**60–65cm**
Maximum size	**3.4m**
Maximum weight	**184kg**
Maturity at	**Male 2.24m** **Female 2.39m**
Reproduction	**Viviparous**
Litter size	**4–17**
Food	**Reef fish and rays, crustaceans and molluscs, on rare occasions also sea birds**
Top speed	**3.2kph**
Teeth count	**54–66**
Depth	**0–92m**

Geographic distribution ■ Confirmed ■ Possible

Manta ray

Manta birostris

Manta ray

Manta birostris

This is the largest batoid or ray with a maximum 'wing' span of 9 metres (average 6.5 metres). Like other rays, the pectoral fins are fused to the head and form large triangular wings, but unlike other rays, the Manta's mouth is at the front of the head instead of below. The tail is short and has no poisonous spines. It has two special fins, one on each side of the mouth that look like horns, to funnel plankton into its mouth. It has a brown to black upper body and a white belly. All Mantas have different markings on both the back and the belly, which are as unique as fingerprints. It has only very small, non-functional teeth in the upper jaw, and eats plankton, krill and some small fish. Manta rays are found worldwide in tropical waters, and they are harmless to humans.

Statistics

Common name	**Manta ray or Devil ray**
Family	**Devil rays**
Size at birth	**1–1.2m (disc width)**
Maximum size	**4m long (without the tail) and 9m wide**
Maximum weight	**3,000kg**
Maturity at	**Male 4m (disc width)** **Female 4.5–5m (disc width)**
Reproduction	**Ovoviviparous**
Litter size	**1–2**
Food	**Plankton, krill and very small fish**
Top speed	**35kph**
Teeth count	**12–18 (lower jaw only)**
Depth	**0–50m**

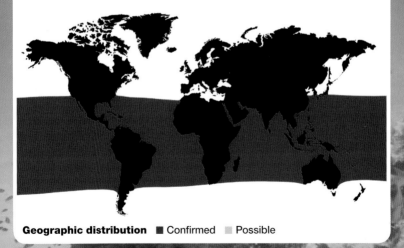

Geographic distribution ■ Confirmed ■ Possible

Marbled Electric ray

Torpedo marmorata

Marbled Electric ray

Torpedo marmorata

This batoid shark has a rounded, disc-shaped body with the pectoral fins fused to the short, thick tail. The upper side is pale brown with dark brown spots and the belly is creamy-white. The teeth are small, smooth-edged cusps. This ray has kidney-shaped organs called narcinoids, which can produce up to 200 volts of electricity. It uses the electricity for defence and for stunning its prey. The Greek name of *Narke* (electric ray) means to stun or paralyse. Marbled Electric rays are found in temperate coastal waters from the southern UK to the southern tip of Africa and also in the Mediterranean. They are generally buried in the sand during the day and hunt bottom-dwelling fish and crustaceans at night. They are potentially dangerous to humans due the risk of electric shock.

Common name	Marbled Electric ray
Family	Torpedo rays
Size at birth	8–12cm
Maximum size	60–65cm (reported to 1m)
Maximum weight	3kg
Maturity at	Male 25–30cm Female 33–36cm
Reproduction	Ovoviviparous
Litter size	5–32
Food	Small bottom-dwelling bony fish and crustaceans
Top speed	Unknown
Teeth count	2
Depth	2–370m

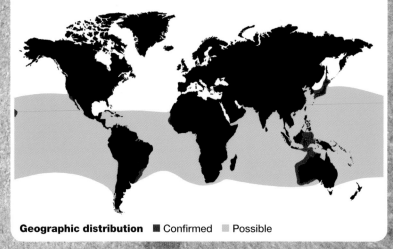

Geographic distribution ■ Confirmed ■ Possible

Megamouth shark

Megachasma pelagios

Megamouth shark

Megachasma pelagios

This is a huge and distinctive shark with a short, broad snout and a very large black mouth. The insides of the gills have 'rakers' (net-like filters) for filtering plankton. The mouth is believed to be luminous, attracting shrimp like a light trap, and has lots of small, hooked teeth. The body is very flabby and is prone to attacks from the Cookie-cutter shark. This is a very rare shark and only approximately 20 specimens have been found, but it is thought to live in warm, deep waters, moving from deep water during the day to shallower water at night. Very little is known about its habits and it is believed only to eat small shrimp, krill, jellyfish and plankton. It is totally harmless to humans.

Common name	Megamouth shark
Family	Megamouth sharks
Size at birth	Unknown
Maximum size	5–6m
Maximum weight	3,500–4,000kg
Maturity at	Male unknown Female approx. 4.7m
Reproduction	Viviparous
Litter size	Unknown but uterine cannibalism is suspected
Food	Plankton, krill and other small shrimp
Top speed	2.1kph
Teeth count	1,000+
Depth	5–4,600m

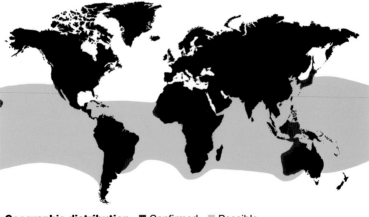

Geographic distribution ■ Confirmed ■ Possible

Oceanic Whitetip shark

Carcharhinus longimanus

Oceanic Whitetip shark

Carcharhinus longimanus

The Oceanic Whitetip is a large stocky shark with a short, broadly rounded snout and small round eyes. The pectoral and dorsal fins are both large with rounded white tips. The upper teeth are broad, triangular and serrated, and the lower teeth are narrower with serrated tips. This shark can be found worldwide in warm to tropical oceanic waters, but sometimes in coastal waters and is one of the most common pelagic sharks. It swims at a very slow pace, but it can also produce short, sharp bursts of speed. This shark feeds on fish, squid, sea birds, turtles, carrion and rubbish. It is believed to be the shark responsible for eating corpses from plane and ship wrecks, and also for attacking and killing the survivors... It is therefore extremely dangerous to swimmers and others sportsmen found on the surface, and approaches divers very closely.

Common name	**Oceanic Whitetip shark**
Family	**Requiem sharks**
Size at birth	**60–65cm**
Maximum size	**3.5–3.95m**
Maximum weight	**167kg**
Maturity at	**Male 1.75–2m** **Female 1.8–2m**
Reproduction	**Viviparous**
Litter size	**1–15**
Food	**Fish, squid, sea birds, turtles, garbage and carrion**
Top speed	**Unknown**
Teeth count	**54–60**
Depth	**0–184m**

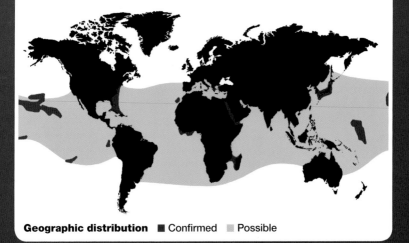

Geographic distribution ■ Confirmed ■ Possible

Pacific Angel shark

Squatina californica

Pacific Angel shark

Squatina californica

The Pacific Angel looks like a batoid, but is in fact a true shark. The pectoral fins are not fused to the head, the gills are on the upper side and the mouth is at the front of the snout. The body is flattened, ray-shaped and pale to white in colour with red, brown and grey blotches. Just like rays, this shark also buries itself in the sand and waits for prey during the day, while at night it hunts by swimming just above the bottom, looking for buried animals. The teeth are pointed and cone-shaped with smooth edges. Pacific Angels are found in the eastern Pacific in tropical to sub-tropical coastal waters, and eat mainly fish but also squid, octopus, molluscs and crabs. They are harmless to humans, but if provoked can inflict very painful deep cuts.

Common name	**Pacific Angel shark**
Family	**Angel sharks**
Size at birth	**23cm**
Maximum size	**1.5m**
Maximum weight	**48kg**
Maturity at	**Male 0.7–0.8m** **Female 0.9–1m**
Reproduction	**Ovoviviparous**
Litter size	**1–13**
Food	**Bony fish, squid, octopus, molluscs and crabs**
Top speed	**Unknown**
Teeth count	**38–40**
Depth	**0–205m**

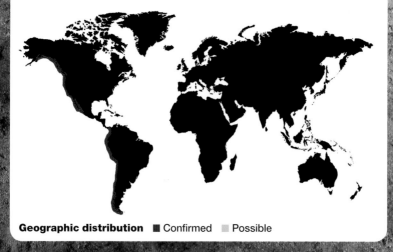

Geographic distribution ■ Confirmed ■ Possible

Port Jackson shark

Heterodontus portusjacksoni

Port Jackson shark

Heterodontus portusjacksoni

This is a small shark with a round body and a large bull head, a pig-shaped nose and spines on both dorsal fins. It also has a unique 'harness' pattern of dark stripes on its back. The teeth are molar-shaped to grind the shell of its prey. This is a nocturnal shark, found in the temperate and sub-tropical inshore waters and coral reefs of Australia, and possibly also in New Zealand. It feeds mainly on sea urchins but also starfish, large gastropods, crustaceans, barnacles and small fish. The female lays 10–12 egg cases which, it is thought, she pushes into crevices with her mouth. The Port Jackson shark is harmless to humans, but can give a nasty nip if annoyed.

Common name	**Port Jackson shark**
Family	**Bullhead sharks**
Size at birth	**23–24cm**
Maximum size	**1.3–1.6m**
Maximum weight	**12kg**
Maturity at	**Male 70–80cm** **Female 80–95cm**
Reproduction	**Oviparous**
Litter size	**10–12**
Food	**Mainly sea urchins, but also starfish, gastropods, crustaceans, polychaetes, barnacles and small fish**
Top speed	**Unknown**
Teeth count	**50–60**
Depth	**5–275m**

Geographic distribution ■ Confirmed ■ Possible

Puffadder Shyshark

Haploblepharus edwardsii

Puffadder Shyshark

Haploblepharus edwardsii

This is a slender shark with a broad head and a nasal flap that extends to the mouth. There are two types of this species: the 'Natal' and the 'Cape', which differ in colour and habitat. It is not known if they are two different species or just colour variations. The 'Cape' form is sandy brown with seven brown, black-bordered saddles and small dark brown and white spots between the saddles, whereas the 'Natal' form is creamy coloured with darker saddles and irregular white spots. The teeth have narrow, pointed cusps and two smaller 'cusplets' (one on each side of the main tooth point) and the female differs in that she has four cusplets (two on each side). It is only found in offshore and inshore waters on sandy and rocky bottoms from Cape Agulhas to Natal, South Africa. It eats bony fish, crustaceans and cephalopods. They are often caught by surf anglers and are harmless to humans.

Common name	**Puffadder Shyshark**
Family	**Catsharks**
Size at birth	**9–10cm**
Maximum size	**59–60cm**
Maximum weight	**35kg**
Maturity at	**Male 42–51cm**
	Female 41–43cm
Reproduction	**Oviparous**
Litter size	**1–2 egg cases**
Food	**Bony fish, crustaceans and cephalopods**
Top speed	**Unknown**
Teeth count	**30–36**
Depth	**0–130m**

Geographic distribution ■ Confirmed ■ Possible

Spotted Ragged-tooth

Carcharias taurus

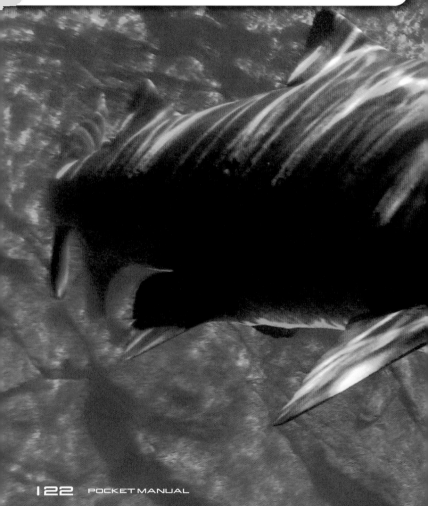

Spotted Ragged-tooth

Carcharias taurus

This is a large and stocky light brown shark with reddish or dark brown spots. The snout is flattish and cone-shaped and the eyes are green. The teeth are long, pointed and dagger-shaped with pointed cusplets to the side of the main tooth point, and stick out from the mouth. Although this shark is heavier than water it is able to 'hover' very still in the water, just above the bottom, by gulping air into its stomach at the surface. It lives worldwide in warm temperate and tropical coastal waters, although not in the central and eastern Pacific and is found either alone or in groups of 60–80. It eats fish, sharks, rays, cephalopods, crustaceans and marine mammals. The female produces 15–25 eggs and uterine cannibalism occurs, resulting in only two pups being born. This is the most common shark to be found in large public aquariums and although harmless to humans, it may bite if annoyed.

Statistics

Common name	**'Raggie' or Spotted Ragged-tooth shark**
Family	**Sand Tiger sharks**
Size at birth	**95–105cm**
Maximum size	**3.2–4.3m**
Maximum weight	**159kg**
Maturity at	**Male 1.9–2m** **Female 2.2–2.5m**
Reproduction	**Ovoviviparous**
Litter size	**2 live pups**
Food	**Fish, sharks, rays, cephalopods, crustaceans and marine mammals**
Top speed	**32kph**
Teeth count	**102–106**
Depth	**0 to at least 200m**

Geographic distribution ■ Confirmed ■ Possible

Salmon shark

Lamna ditropis

Common name	**Salmon shark**
Family	**Mackerel sharks**
Size at birth	**84–96cm**
Maximum size	**3.5–3.7m**
Maximum weight	**450kg**
Maturity at	**Male 1.77–1.86m** **Female 2–2.3m**
Reproduction	**Ovoviviparous**
Litter size	**1–4**
Food	**Pelagic salmon, trout and other large bony fish**
Speed	**80kph**
Teeth count	**56–60**
Depth	**0–152m**

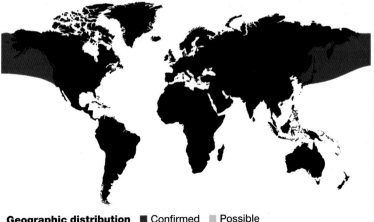

Geographic distribution ■ Confirmed ■ Possible

Sixgill Sawshark

Pliotrema warreni

Sixgill Sawshark

Pliotrema warreni

This is a fairly small, flattish shark with six gill slits, an elongated snout with sawteeth and barbels. It has two spineless dorsal fins and no anal fins. Its teeth are broad with smooth, pointed cusps. The barbels on its snout are possibly used to detect prey in the sand by sense of 'taste'. The snout is also filled with sensory organs to detect buried animals. It is found in the tropical to sub-tropical deep waters of the western Indian Ocean, mainly concentrated along the south-eastern coast of South Africa and Madagascar. It eats fish, squid and crustaceans and is believed to use its saw to catch prey by shaking its head from side to side in schools of fish and squid. The dead or injured prey can then be eaten at leisure. It is considered harmless to humans.

Statistics

Common name	**Sixgill Sawshark**
Family	**Sawsharks**
Size at birth	**30–35cm**
Maximum size	**1.3–1.4m**
Maximum weight	**350kg**
Maturity at	**Male 80–85cm** **Female 1–1.1m**
Reproduction	**Ovoviviparous**
Litter size	**5–17**
Food	**Small fish, squid and crustaceans**
Top speed	**Unknown**
Teeth count	**50–64**
Depth	**50–450m**

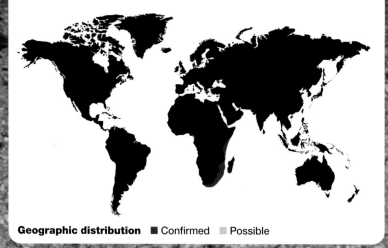

Geographic distribution ■ Confirmed ■ Possible

Scalloped Hammerhead

Sphyrna lewini

Scalloped Hammerhead

Sphyrna lewini

The Scalloped Hammerhead is a large, bulky shark with a broad, narrow-bladed head full of sensory organs and with the eyes located at each end of the blade. It swims while swinging its head and this is thought to help it to see and sense things around it. Its teeth are fairly broad with smooth or slightly serrated edges. This shark can be found worldwide in warm to tropical coastal waters and is very common. It is often found in large schools, such as above the seamounts (underwater monutains) off southern Baja California. It feeds on a large range of different species, including fish, squid, crustaceans, rays and other smaller sharks. It is potentially dangerous to humans although attacks are more likely to be by its larger cousin, the Great Hammerhead.

Common name	Scalloped Hammerhead shark
Family	Hammerhead sharks
Size at birth	42–55cm
Maximum size	3.7–4.2m
Maximum weight	152kg
Maturity at	Male 1.4m Female 2.2m
Reproduction	Viviparous
Litter size	15–31 in litter
Food	Fish, squid, octopus, conger eels, crabs, mantis shrimps, rays, other smaller sharks
Top speed	40kph
Teeth count	64–78
Depth	0–275m

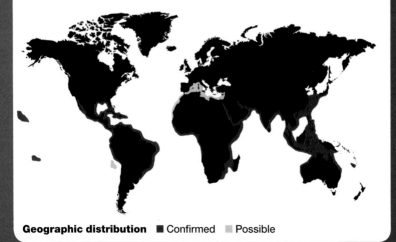

Geographic distribution ■ Confirmed ■ Possible

Shortfin Mako shark

Isurus oxyrhincus

Shortfin Mako shark

Isurus oxyrhincus

This is a large, round shark with a very pointed, cone-shaped snout and a crescent-shaped tail. The upper side is dark to metallic blue with a snow-white belly. Its teeth are long and blade-like with smooth edges and stick out from the mouth. It is a very fast and aggressive shark – maybe the fastest shark alive – and will often leap three to four body lengths high out of the water. It is warm-blooded, with a body temperature between 1–15 degrees Celsius higher than the surrounding water. It is found worldwide in tropical to sub-tropical waters (above 17 degrees Celsius) mostly in pelagic, open ocean areas but sometimes it will come also to inshore waters. It eats all pelagic fish, cephalopods and smaller sharks. It is not known to attack humans, but many divers have reported Makos shooting towards them at high speed only to veer off at the last second, maybe playing 'chicken'.

Silky shark

Carcharhinus falciformis

This is a long, slim, dark-grey shark with a long, rounded snout and fairly large eyes. It has no special markings, but it has long thin 'strands' behind the two dorsal fins at the base. The teeth are triangular and heavily serrated in the upper jaw, and narrow and thin with no serrations in the lower jaw. It is found globally in tropical offshore, oceanic waters and sometimes near coastal islands. It is a very fast and aggressive swimmer, but tends to give way to the slower and bulkier Oceanic Whitetip when they meet. It is known as the 'net-eater shark' because of the damage it does when ripping open tuna nets to get at the fish. It eats all pelagic fish, especially yellow fin tuna but also squid and pelagic crabs. This shark is potentially dangerous to humans and will approach divers, although no attacks have ever been reported. It displays a hunch-back pose when threatened.

Common name	Silky shark
Family	Requiem sharks
Size at birth	70–87cm
Maximum size	3.3m
Maximum weight	346kg
Maturity at	Male 1.9–2.2m Female 2.1–2.3m
Reproduction	Viviparous
Litter size	2–14
Food	Plankton, krill and possibly other small fish
Top speed	Unknown
Teeth count	70–74
Depth	0–500m

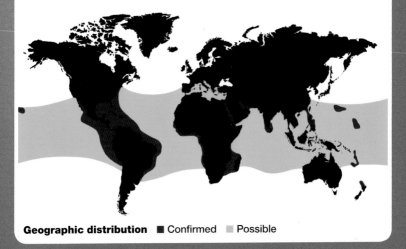

Geographic distribution ■ Confirmed ■ Possible

Silvertip shark

Carcharhinus albimarginatus

Silvertip shark

Carcharhinus albimarginatus

The Silvertip is very similar in size and shape to the Silky shark, but has distinctive white tips and edges to all fins. The teeth are also similar except that the tooth root is much broader and the serrations on the upper teeth are much coarser. It is found in tropical inshore and offshore waters in the Indian and Pacific oceans, Red Sea and Gulf of Mexico. Sightings in the Caribbean have not been confirmed. It is not a true oceanic shark, preferring coral reefs and drop-offs around islands and coastal shelves. It eats midwater and bottom-dwelling fish, octopus and eagle rays. It is very aggressive towards other sharks and darts in to steal fish while they are feeding. Although considered dangerous to humans due to its large size and aggressive behaviour, no confirmed reports of attacks exist. However, in an experiment with a dummy dressed in diving gear a Silvertip was annoyed and it tore off the dummy's leg...

Common name	**Silvertip shark**
Family	**Requiem sharks**
Size at birth	**63–68cm**
Maximum size	**3m**
Maximum weight	**162kg**
Maturity at	**Male 1.6–1.8m** **Female 1.6–2m**
Reproduction	**Viviparous**
Litter size	**1–11**
Food	**Midwater and bottom-dwelling fish, octopus and eagle rays**
Top speed	**Unknown**
Teeth count	**48–56**
Depth	**0–800m**

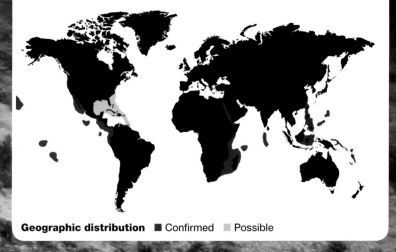

Geographic distribution ■ Confirmed ■ Possible

Spotted Eagle ray

Aetobatus narinari

Spotted Eagle ray

Aetobatus narinari

The Spotted Eagle ray is a batoid (not a true shark). The pectoral fins are fused to the head and are large and wing-shaped. It has a very long whip tail that counts for two-thirds of the shark's length, with several poisonous, barbed spines at the base. The body is grey, yellow or brown with white to bluish-white spots. The snout is broad and long with a medium-sized mouth. The face looks a bit like that of a mouse. The teeth are two 'plates' used for crushing shells. It also has six to eight papillae (fleshy finger-type appendages) in the mouth for removing shell debris. It eats crustaceans, molluscs, snails, sea urchins, squid and small bony fish. The Spotted Eagle ray is found worldwide in tropical waters on coral reefs with sandy patches, sandy lagoons and estuaries. Due to its long 'whip' and poisonous barbs, it is potentially dangerous to humans.

Common name	**Spotted Eagle ray**
Family	**Whiptail rays**
Size at birth	**17–35cm**
Maximum size	**7–9m long and 2.5–3m wide**
Maximum weight	**230kg**
Maturity at	**Male n/a** **Female n/a**
Reproduction	**Ovoviviparous**
Litter size	**4**
Food	**Molluscs, crustaceans, snails, sea urchins, squid and small bony fish**
Top speed	**Unknown**
Teeth count	**2**
Depth	**2–80m**

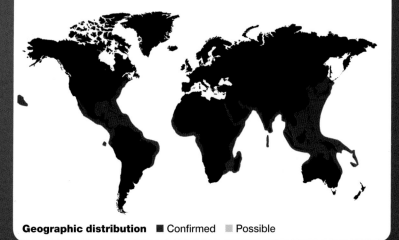

Geographic distribution ■ Confirmed ■ Possible

Starry Smooth-hound

Mustelus asterias

Starry Smooth-hound

Mustelus asterias

This is a medium-sized, slender grey shark with white spotted markings. It has large, oval eyes and a slightly angular snout (seen from the side), an unfringed dorsal fin (unlike most other sharks) and smallish pectoral and pelvic fins. Its teeth are small and molar-shaped with small pointed cusps in a curved mouth that ends behind the eyes. It is a very common shark found between northern Scotland, all around the British Isles down to Mauritania and also in the Mediterranean Sea, generally in shallow waters over sandy or shingle bottoms but also in deeper waters and occasionally in midwater. Due to the fact that it prefers to swim near the bottom, it is often caught in bottom-trawling nets in huge numbers. It eats lobsters, crabs and snails. It is harmless to humans, but is eaten in large numbers by humans.

Common name	**Starry Smooth-hound**
Family	**Hound sharks**
Size at birth	**25–30cm**
Maximum size	**1.4m**
Maximum weight	**5kg**
Maturity at	**Male 75–85cm** **Female 85–90cm**
Reproduction	**Viviparous**
Litter size	**7–15**
Food	**Crustaceans and snails**
Top speed	**Unknown**
Teeth count	**Unknown**
Depth	**5 to at least 100m**

Geographic distribution ■ Confirmed ■ Possible

Tasselled Wobbegong

Eucrossorhinus dasypogon

Tasselled Wobbegong

Eucrossorhinus dasypogon

This is a unique species of carpet shark, slightly similar only to the Angel shark. However, unlike Angel sharks, Wobbegongs have anal fins. They have broad, flattened heads and bodies with distinct branched lateral skin flaps around the snout and their dorsal fins are spineless. Their bodies have distinct mosaic camouflage markings. The teeth are dagger-shaped medium cusps. These ambush predators are found on coral reefs, where they hide camouflaged ready to suck in their prey. They are thought to be nocturnal, hiding in caves and underhangs during the day. The mouth is huge and has the power of several vacuum cleaners. Wobbegongs are found in the south-western Pacific in tropical waters. They eat bony fish, crustaceans, cephalopods and other benthic animals. They are harmless to humans but if trodden on will bite. They are capable of removing a foot or leg, so should be treated with respect.

Common name	Tasselled Wobbegong shark
Family	Wobbegongs
Size at birth	20–25cm
Maximum size	2.5–3m
Maximum weight	Unknown
Maturity at	Male 1.1–1.2m Female 1.1–1.4m?
Reproduction	Ovoviviparous
Litter size	At least 20
Food	Bony fish, squid, octopus, molluscs and crabs
Top speed	Unknown
Teeth count	41–49
Depth	2–50m

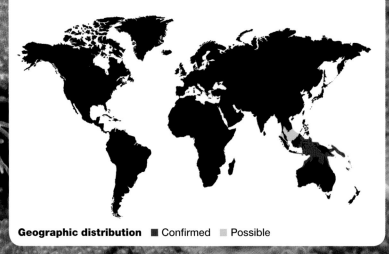

Geographic distribution ■ Confirmed ■ Possible

Tawny Nurse shark

Nebrius ferrugineus

SHARKS 159

Tawny Nurse shark

Nebrius ferrugineus

This is a failry large bottom-dwelling shark, grey to brown in colour. It has nasal grooves with barbles on each side and a straight, narrow mouth. Its first dorsal fin is positioned far back on the body above the pelvic fins and the tail is approximately one-quarter of the body length. It is found in tropical inshore waters of the west Indo-Pacific oceans, Australia, China, Japan and west Asia. Its teeth are broad with a short cusp and 10–12 lateral cusplets (to the side of the main cusp). These are nocturnal sharks, found resting on the bottom or in groups lying on top of each other in caves during the day. It eats corals, crustaceans, sea urchins, squid and small fish, which it sucks into its mouth like a giant vacuum cleaner. It is harmless to humans, but will bite if annoyed. However, this shark is able to reverse the suction method it uses for eating to blast water into the face of its captors and therefore it could be considered potentially dangerous.

Statistics

Common name	**Tawny Nurse shark**
Family	**Nurse sharks**
Size at birth	**40–60cm**
Maximum size	**3.14–3.2m**
Maximum weight	**150kg**
Maturity at	**Male 2.5m** **Female 2.3–2.8m**
Reproduction	**Ovoviviparous with uterine cannibalism**
Litter size	**1–4 egg cases**
Food	**Crustaceans, corals, squid, sea urchins and small bony fish**
Top speed	**Unknown**
Teeth count	**46–54**
Depth	**0 to at least 70m**

Geographic distribution ■ Confirmed ■ Possible

Thresher shark

Alopias pelagicus

Thresher shark

Alopias pelagicus

This is a long, slender shark with a pointed snout and round eyes. The upper lobe of the tail is distinctively long and is equal to the length of the body. The teeth are small with small cusplets behind the main triangular cusp on upper teeth, with the cusplets being more rounded on the lower teeth. It is found in the tropical oceanic waters of the Indo-Pacific Ocean but also in the Red Sea and Gulf of California. It is a very active swimmer, preferring open pelagic waters, but also sometimes near offshore reefs and islands. It is assumed to feed on fish and squid and it is also believed to use the long tail to 'thresh' into large schools of fish, stunning them so they can be caught easily. Thresher sharks are harmless to humans.

Common name	**Pelagic Thresher shark**
Family	**Thresher sharks**
Size at birth	**96cm**
Maximum size	**3.3m**
Maximum weight	**69kg**
Maturity at	**Male 2.76m** **Female 2.64m**
Reproduction	**Ovoviviparous with uterine cannibalism**
Litter size	**2–3**
Food	**Small fish and Squid**
Top speed	**At least 48kph**
Teeth count	**84–88**
Depth	**0–152m**

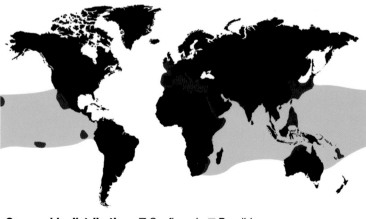

Geographic distribution ■ Confirmed ■ Possible

Tiger shark

Galeocerdo cuvier

Tiger shark

Galeocerdo cuvier

This is a huge, stocky shark with a broad, blunt snout and distinctive vertical tiger stripes. It has a large mouth and the large teeth are cockscomb-shaped (like the crest of a cock's head) with heavily serrated saw-like edges and rear cusplets. It can be found worldwide in tropical and temperate waters, and also in river estuaries, and close inshore near docks, jetties and harbours. It eats anything and is known as the swimming rubbish bin – trainers, backpacks and even a suit of armour have been found in Tiger shark stomachs! Normally, though, it eats seals, turtles, sea birds, sea snakes, crustaceans, dolphins, fish and other sharks. It is generally a nocturnal shark, although young Tigers may be more active in the day than adults. The Tiger shark is extremely dangerous to humans, and is recorded as having attacked and re-attacked humans, boats and surfboards. It is number two in the shark attack files, although it should be number one as most attacks reported to be by Great Whites are more likely to be by Tiger sharks.

Common name	**Tiger shark**
Family	**Requiem sharks**
Size at birth	**51–76cm**
Maximum size	**5–7m**
Maximum weight	**807kg**
Maturity at	**Male 2.3–2.9m** **Female 2.5–3.5m**
Reproduction	**Ovoviviparous**
Litter size	**10–82**
Food	**Marine mammals, reptiles, birds, fish, rays, crustaceans, sharks, garbage and carrion**
Top speed	**At least 3.8kph**
Teeth count	**36–52**
Depth	**0–140m**

Geographic distribution ■ Confirmed ■ Possible

Whale shark

Rhincodon typus

Whale shark

Rhincodon typus

The Whale shark is an unmistakable and extremely large grey shark with unique white dots and stripes on its body and fins. It has a large, broad head and mouth, which contains more than 300 rows of tiny teeth and gills that are much larger than normal, with extra filter screens on the inside slits. This is one of the three plankton-feeding sharks and is found worldwide in warm temperate and tropical, coastal and oceanic waters and even coral reef lagoons. Generally, Whale sharks swim just below the surface and they have been tagged and followed by satellites over distances of more than 3,500 kilometres over a period of five months. This is a curious shark, approaching divers, snorklers and boats to 'check them out'. It is totally harmless to humans, although a bump from its tail will hurt!

Common name	Whale shark
Family	Whale sharks
Size at birth	58–64cm
Maximum size	16–18m
Maximum weight	35,800kg
Maturity at	Male 5–6m Female 6–8m
Reproduction	Ovoviviparous
Litter size	Up to 300 in litter
Food	Plankton, krill and other small fish
Top speed	9.7kph
Teeth count	300+
Depth	0–700m

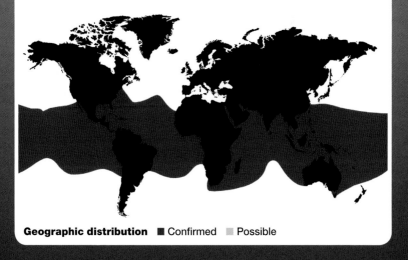

Geographic distribution ■ Confirmed ■ Possible

Whitespotted Bamboo

Chiloscyllium plagiosum

Whitespotted Bamboo

Chiloscyllium plagiosum

This is a small, slender bamboo shark with a stout body and tail. It has unique dark saddle markings with light, white or blue spots on its brown body. Its upper tail fin is long with a notch just before the tip. The teeth are medium cusps with tiny cusplets. It is found in tropical, shallow, inshore waters in the Indo-Pacific and Madagascar, although the Madagascan one is believed to be another species. Although often found in aquariums, little is known about the habits of this shark in the wild. It generally hides under corals during the day and emerges to hunt at night. When moving in the reef, it either swims just above the bottom or it hops on its flexible pectoral fins. It feeds on small bony fish and their hatchlings, squid, mussels and snails. It is harmless to humans.

Common name	**Whitespotted Bamboo shark**
Family	**Bamboo sharks**
Size at birth	**14–16cm**
Maximum size	**95–100cm**
Maximum weight	**29kg**
Maturity at	**Male 50–65cm** **Female 75–80cm**
Reproduction	**Oviparous**
Litter size	**Unknown number of egg cases**
Food	**Small bony fish and larvae, squid, mussels and snails**
Top speed	**Unknown**
Teeth count	**21–35**
Depth	**0–30m**

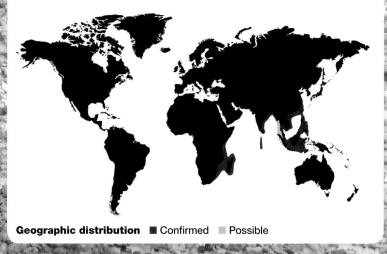

Geographic distribution ■ Confirmed ▪ Possible

Whitetip Reef shark

Triaenodon obesus

Whitetip Reef shark

Triaenodon obesus

This is a small, slender grey shark with very distinct white tips on its first and second dorsal fins and also on the upper tail fin. Its teeth have narrow and triangular cusps and two lateral cusplets. The lower jaw teeth have thicker roots, but the base of the tooth is narrower than the upper jaw teeth. It is often seen lying on the bottom or resting in caves during the day, but at night it becomes very active, squeezing itself between the corals to feed on sleeping fish and octopus. For this reason, it has a very thick protective skin to prevent it being cut by the sharp corals. It can be found in the tropical waters of the coral reefs and island shelves in the Red Sea, Indian and Pacific Oceans, Australia, Asia, Polynesia and western Central America. It is harmless to humans.

Common name	**Whitetip Reef shark**
Family	**Requiem sharks**
Size at birth	**52–60cm**
Maximum size	**1.6–2.1m**
Maximum weight	**20kg**
Maturity at	**Male 1–1.05m**
	Female 1–1.1m
Reproduction	**Viviparous**
Litter size	**1–5**
Food	**Small reef fish, crustaceans and octopus**
Top speed	**Unknown**
Teeth count	**91–96**
Depth	**0–110m**

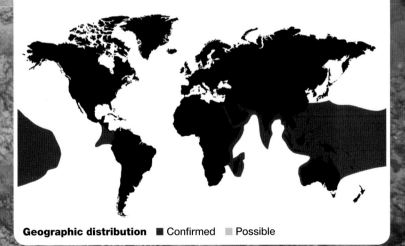

Geographic distribution ■ Confirmed ▨ Possible

Zebra shark
or Leopard Nurse shark
Stegostoma fasciatum

Zebra shark

or Leopard Nurse shark

Stegostoma fasciatum

This is a unique large shark, with a round body, ridges on its back and a long tail, almost the same length as the rest of the shark. It has nasal grooves with barbles on each side and a straight, narrow mouth. It is black with yellow zebra stripes when young and has a leopard-spotted coat when mature. It is found in tropical inshore waters of the west Indo-Pacific oceans, Australia, China, Japan and west Asia. Its teeth are small and trident-shaped (three-pronged) with a tall, pointed cusp and two lateral pointed cusplets. It is generally found resting on the sand between corals facing the current in the day and is assumed to be more active during the night. It eats snails and mussels, crabs, shrimps and small fish. The female lays one to four egg cases with hair-like tufts that anchor the case to the reef. It is harmless to humans. However, if annoyed, it will bite and then hold on like a bull dog. Climbing out of the water is difficult with a large shark attached to your leg!

Common name	Zebra shark or Leopard Nurse shark
Family	Zebra sharks
Size at birth	20–36cm
Maximum size	3.6m (half of which is tail!)
Maximum weight	215kg
Maturity at	Male 1.5–1.8m Female 1.7–1.8m
Reproduction	Oviparous
Litter size	1–4 egg cases
Food	Molluscs, crustaceans and small bony fish
Top speed	Unknown
Teeth count	50–64
Depth	0 to at least 50m

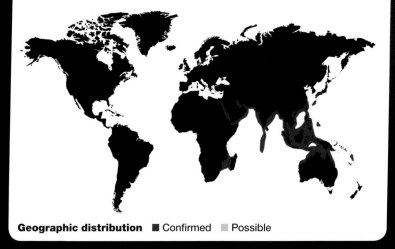

Geographic distribution ■ Confirmed ■ Possible